Still I Stand

Still I Stand

Brianna V. Payne

"It's easy to make mistakes, but its hard to learn from them,
once you learn from them it'll make you stronger.

To order additional copies of this book, contact:
Xlibris Corporation
1-888-795-4274
www.Xlibris.com
Orders@Xlibris.com
72695

Contents

Why

Why go after things you can't have?

Why say things you dont mean?

Why look around for trouble you can't handle?

Why put your head down when people down grade you?

Why do people fear other humans?

Why do people kill one another and innocents?

Why do people comitte suicide?

Why do females get a reputation?

Why std's can't be cured?

Why do you have to be a certain person to get respect?

Why people can't love you for who you are?

Why?

Why ask questions, when i can't get an answer too.

Crying Myself to Sleep

Sitting here alone in bed,

wishing there was certain things i said

Try to think about the good times,

but all there is . . . .

Is the bad times

I wanna let my anger out

I wanna sit in certain places and shout

Don't wanna have a future of hell

Don't wanna be young living in jail

Tears falling down my eyes,

there's nothing but guilt and lies while

i'm crying myself to sleep.

Disrespect

What you did to me was

disrespectful

You ripped my heart out and

threw it away

You made me disrespect everyone

around me

You made me not care

anymore

You made me leave my home

You made me not talk about

my situation and

when I do

You made me feel like it wont never

go away

i've disrespected people that never ever hurt me

because you disrespected me in hurtful ways

I HATE YOU !

Can You Love Me

She runs down the hall crying her eyes out, while people laugh in her face.

She runs fast as she could but every corner she reaches there's laughter here and there.

She's home from school, runs straight to her room, as she looks up she's down on both knees with both hands together, as she talks to god.

"Why do i look like this?"

"Look like what, a beautiful young women"

"No, like this"

God look down at her and replied,

"My angel you are differen't, no ones alike"

She ask god to help her,

"No not with this, you have to help yourself, or either deal with it people are going to be people"

"God what should i do?"

"Nothing, but ignore it all"

"God can you love me so i won't feel like im not loved"

"Finally, yes my darling, your my child and that's one thing i do best is love you and everyone else"

"thank you my father god, thank you"

Love was what she got,hatetrate was what she ignored.

So she stand with her head held high while her smile brightens the rest of her night and days.

What is it Really About

It's not about you being my mother friend or about you tryna make other people happy,

it's about respect, about you respecting my sister body and mines, and why you touching our body in the wrong places.

About me being fourteen years old and her being nine. Being abused by a grown man

It's about you putting your hands on us

about us thinking about this horrible situation and

me blaming it on everyone else

when it was your fault,

about me disrespecting my mom after this situation

when she was trying to help me and my sister,

it's about you sexually assulting us

thats what it's really about,

so i ask myself and wishing i could ask you

why?

Leave Me Alone

There she go, there he go, bothering me from
time to time, leave me alone, say no more i
can't take this all on my back oh my gosh leave
me alone
Minding my business and you still on my back.
Back off go ahead, over there over here, still on
my back, so much built up inside me. go your
way and leave me alone.

Struggle

Living with so much struggle

Living with so much hurt

Filled with an angry bubble

Wishing it would go away

What do I do

Only because your not here my heart begins to crack.

So much anger and fear, what do I do when my hero is gone.

Here alone feels like I have no one here, what do I do when the aunt I love so dearly say her last goodbye, her last

"I Love You" blink her eye one last time, what do I do when

I cry everyday for her but she drop that one last tear that I could never see again or feel how wet it is when I wipe it away,

what do I do when

I can't hear her beautiful voice saying

"I Love You"

What do I do when I ask a question that I can't get the correct answer too.

What do you do?

I don't know because i'm still trying to figure out what do i do.

What's Going to Happen Next

In the middle of the night
August 30th 2003,sleeping,
moreless I just didn't hear
I'm in one bed my sister in the other
Our twin brother and sister sleep on each of the
bed my second born sister stayed over a friend
While mommy at work all night long
Kitchen glass window breaking
sleeping so tight you couldn't hear
nothing laying on my stomach something
heavy leaning back on my back
waking up with no fear, I recgonize the face
"Where's your mom" he asked
"she's at work" I replied
paying no attention to the situation of why he's here when mommy at work
Fallin back to sleep not knowing what's
going to happen next few minutes later something
rubbing against her 14 year old body, scared, shaking
STOP, STOP, MOVE she said
Leaving the room going to the next
Knocking stuff over as I still have that fear in
my heart, my body, so scared, heart pounding
so fast and breaking apart
Entering the room again sitting on my
sister bed, back and fourth from bed to bed touching that 14 and 9 year
old body as i hold my little brother tight
Come over here bring baby girl. He left out the house,
mommy bused in an hour later because the door was unlock,
running towards the back room i'm up in bed crying telling her what happen
Scared to leave my room, my bed. We run
outside as she stopped a car to use the phone,
cops coming up, going down to the police station not really wanting to talk
Explaining
my story with so much fear in my heart, close so, so close to getting rap
thank you god i wasn't.
Being sexually assulted with a half million dollar bail bond.

The Last GoOdbye

It was a laugh
that i could never forget.
That one last laugh
that made everyone happy

It was that last I love you
that had a smile on everyone face
that i love you had everyone sayin
i love you

The first and last hero
who saved you from getting hurt
that first and last hero
who said they'll be there forever

It was the last joke she said
that had people dying for weeks
that last joke put joy in everyone heart

it was that last
tear drop you took
that made everyone
cry with you

That last goodbye you waved
at us as we all stayed and
didn't want to see you
go forever

But that last breath you took went to the edge
that last breath you took broke everyone heart
that last breath you took had me crying for weeks
that last goodbye

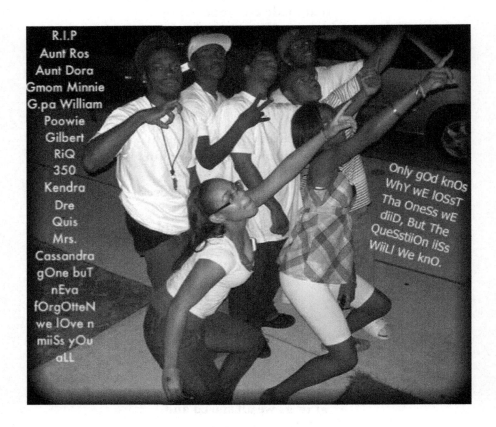

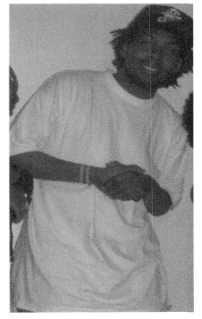

~ Life ~

Life is a struggle, life is pain, life is a mix up, life is
ashame
Where do you go when there's no one around, where do
you go when everything seems so empty and dark. Black
everywhere i can't see nothing. Who do you call on when everyone is
gone.
Who do you look up to when your
hero isn't there.
Life is a struggle, life is pain, life is a mix up, life is
ashame. Break down in tears no where to go, no one to call on,
eyes bloody red, feet burning out, hands cramping up,
it's so dark out here no light no where, no voices but the echo of mines.
Where do i go? Where do i go?
So much pain it's ashame, so much struggle it's a mix up
it's crazy cause it's life.

Our Love Remain

I was sitting home alone when I heard a knock at de
door. Long time no see, jumpng up with excitment,
remeber the days we spent together the laughs we
shared the kisses we blew oh those times were perfect,
then we lost eachother but what seperated our love?
my love still remain for this fly boy. so in love with you
I dont regret being with you.
The way you held my hands when we walked the streets,
the way you kissed me in
public letting people kno I was your girl,
your my other half. Always and forever our love have
remain the same. I love you, I love you, I love you my darling.

est.03(Cary M Little)

Many mix personalities in this world,
what to think? what to do? happy moments,
sad moment, silly moment and just weird moments
am i weird was what they ask me, i don't know, am i ?
i sat on my bed and decided to write something in this little
diary of mines

Dear Diary,
would i be weird if i write
about leaves something funny,
i'm not always sad i think i'm funny too:

Leaves

Ch ch ch ch ch ch ch ch
walking on them crunchy leaves,
ch ch ch ch ch ch
Fall if here, flowers are leaving,
ch ch ch ch ch
Leaves, leaves, leaves so
colorful and bright
beautiful orange,
the yellow so wonderful,
so so nice ch ch ch ch
stepping on the beautiful crunchy leaves

I Understand

Waking up in the middle of the night
just wondering where my life is headed.
Trying to figure out who i am. Acting a fool
Breaking all the rules,
Not caring what people say about me,
Getting suspended from school.
Shedding tears with my little siblings
Not much love for my daddy cause he was really never there.
Momma never turned her back
it was hard for her to raise five kids
Especially when the two oldest were the baddest.
No matter what my momma will always be appreciated
for what she's done.
Fighting everyday and everyone that gave me a dirty look,
tryna be a thug girl the most gangsta one on the block.
I've always loved Tupac and what he said was true
"if you could make it through the night there's a brighter day"
I can't pay you back but i do understand
and you are appreciated.

Life apart from you is hurting

why i need this
living life like this so young
i can't live like this

when your hero leave
what do you do when their gone?
i need my only hero

Together forever we will be
life ahead of us long lasting
until death do us part

9-1-07

Sometimes you sit back
and wonder was it all a dream,
until tears drop from your eyes
and you feel that it's really wet
and on the tip of your finger.
when everything starting to
change about you.
You sit back and wonder was it all a dream
until you read the news paper
telling all the facts.
Sit back and wonder was it all a dream
until you step in the church
looking at people crying a river.
You sit back and wonder until it all
hit you in the face that it wasn't a dream.
So you cry tears of joy because the fun times ya'll had
but tears of sadness because your not around no more.
A good friend disappeared so fast
that you couldn't even get the chance
to say
good bye.

R.I.P Gilbert

Chapter 1

Story of her Life

She Was born in Burlington New Jersey a little place call Burlington City. She had so many family and friends she lefted behind but she guess seeing her mother dealing with something that couldn't be controlled we had to go. At age nine she moved to Greenville North Carolina. Greenville was a lovely place she would call home but never did she forget about her home town Burlington City. Being raised in Greenville She meet a lot of new friends but she was always quiet and in her own little world. Never did she played with many people because she was always the outcast of any group. She was always picked on for some reason but had many people that liked her a lot. She grew up with two siblings Tawanna and Tylicia a mother who loved her dearly, Felicia.

Year 2000 Felicia had two little ones, twins they were, Nicholas and Niesha. After a year or two she moved around the corner on Green St from Authur St living with her Aunt Dora who took them in after moving from New Jersey down to North Carolina. Two years later the family moved into the most countriest part in North Carolina Blvd. After starting school there was when a lot of enemies came alone, many people who disliked her and picked wit her but that didn't stop her from keeping her head held high.

In 2003 the family moved back into Greenville on 4th St. It was 2003 summer her cousins from New Jersey Came down to visit for the whole summer. In Felicia home there was a full house of kids. Gary, Brianna, Malik, Tawanna, Marniqua, Tylicia, Mikea, and then the twins Nicholas and Niesha, with a three bed room but they all manage to have fun, and plus having friends over everyday was just the best part of the summer. August 29th was the night my family from New Jersey came alone to pick the kids up from their summer break.

August 30th around 1am in the middle of the night everyone would be sleeping or well thats what she thought. Tylicia slept on the bed with her little sister Niesha, as Brianna slept on the other bed with her little brother Nicholas. The bed room was a very big room enough to fit two queen size bed in. Tawanna had stayed out that night over a family member home, but all night mommy was at work. Glass window shattering but in a deep sleep the kids never heard a sound. There was something heavy lying on

Brianna back as she jumped up with no fear in her mind but not thinking anything of the situation of why Joe would lean back on her back while she's sleeping.

"Where's your mom" he asked
"she's at work" Brianna replied

as she falls back to sleep not thinking about anything but her rest that she would have loved to continue if she wasn't touch in different places by a filthy man who she hated but still loved in many ways and people asked her why?

In September Brianna meet a guy who she knew would keep her going. Cary was something special to her but someone years older than her. Cary was seventeen but at that time Brianna was to in love. Did she really knew what love was at fourteen? He made her feel like he was the only one that knew her. his family was great to her and loved her dearly but love had to run away. The only person she could count on and who made her feel like she didn't have to worry about pain anymore was her best friend Tynisha who she loved and cared about so dearly.

October Brianna was picked up by her Aunt Dee who came all the way from New Jersey to welcome her into a better home a better environment. Brianna didn't want to leave North Carolina, giving her mother a hard time wasnt the best thing for her nor her mother Felicia. A lot of things got worse but living with the worse things only came out to be the better things in life. Moving back to Jersey with her Aunt Dee in Township Brianna meets many people well being as though her cousin Malik and Gary was known by everyone a lot of people respected her and welcomed her into their lives. Living with her Aunt Dee, her kids and my wonderful Grandmother Clara, she had to make it work. Brianna was never the outside person after moving back to Jersey she stayed home at all times until she got reunited with her friend Sheree and her cousin Danicqua who she love so dearly. By staying five minutes away from Burlington City living in township was the worst because in walking distance it had to be a twenty minute walk until you get use to it. After a while living in Township and going to the school Brianna meet this one guy name Ravon and Rendal they were more like the best male friends she had. Rendal was the funniest guy she had ever meet besides her cousin Malik. Ravon was her first kiss but also a good friend as well. Things gotten better with Brianna but things were alot stressful for her, missing home her mother and her siblings wasn't just the best idea for her to up and leave her loved ones. After spending a year in Burlington New Jersey, Brianna moved back to Greenville North Carolina with her family in 2004. Moving back made her feel so happy. Things gotten a lot better for her, after living in a town where she was hurt so much she decided not to care about life anymore nor the people who tried to make it better for her. In 2004 as the minutes turn into hours and the hours turned into days the days turned into weeks and the weeks turned into months as Brianna behavior just gotten worse, but why? was the question they asked her and the question she asked her self. Summer 2004 right before Brianna turned sixteen she decided to get worse and worse. Running away from home was the most regretted decision she made. While walking around at a young age anything could've happened to her, in her mind she was OK if she had to go that night there's was nothing she could've done. Walking until her foot took her to a stop. someone drove up behind Brianna but frightened? she wasn't.

"You look to young to be walking out here, how old are you?" a stranger asked
"i'm only fifteen"
"get in the car, i have a little sister your age and i would beat her down if she was out here this time of night"
"I don't know you i'm not getting in your car"
So Brianna continues to walk away from the car but he continues his conversation with Brianna

"Listen sweetie i'm not from around here, i'm not going to do anything to you, your to young to be out here it's 1am"

Brianna decided to get in the car, she thought to her self if her life was going to be taking that night then so be it. As this stranger drove her around he threw a lot of decisions in her head that she had to think about either now or whenever.

"Look your to pretty to be out here' i'm not going to do anything to you but i hate to see you out here this late."

he pointed at two young males and a drug addict. As Brianna looked, well thats all she could do.

"Now that drug addict see a young lady walking out this time a night what you think might happen he lives on these streets, and i'm sure he hasn't have a girlfriend in years so think about what he might do, and them two young boys over there they don't care about you they probably would have stopped you and did whatever without thinking twice."

All she could do is cry for her life, even though this strange guy was telling her something true, she didn't know him.

"if i drove down this dark rode to where ever what would you do, i mean i'm not from around here so don't nobody know me, where are you going to go if i just drove to where ever" he asked
"I don't know"
"i'm going to take you home, you don't have to go there but i hate to look at the news and see you as one of these missing kids, either you go in or sleep on your porch its the safest place to be"

As Brianna takes him to her near by neighborhood, she gets out the car and said

"thank you Rico"
Brianna goes home and knocks on the door as her mom opens the door and lets her in, all she could do was cry and leaves towards her room. That night Brianna mother tells her she got to go tomorrow. Brianna followed her rules and left. She had no where to go. One family that she could count on was her ex boyfriend mother Mrs. Inez, who took her in with no hesitation. Cary wasn't home he had moved to D.C while Brianna was staying in New jersey. After two days staying there Nick who was the twins father and my grandmother Clara had came to North Carolina unexpected by Brianna. She decides to take it upon herself and not listen to what they were saying to her. about an hour later Nick decides to try and bring Brianna back home to her mother but she wasn't taking no chances on going back. There was a big conflict between Brianna and Nick to where a lot of swinging was going on. the neighborhood watched but couldn't really do anything. A few days after Nick and grand-mom Clara leaves to go back to Jersey, Aunt Dee decides to come back to North Carolina to pick Brianna up for a second round. Brianna had know choice but to leave.
Back in Jersey back in township schools. She meet a good friend name Alleah who treated her so well with no hesitation she took her heart and

gave it to Brianna along with her mother Kim. Brianna Fell in love with them and spent every moment in their home. At age sixteen Brianna meets this guy Pierre who no one in school really liked but her. She had one of the most biggest crush on him. They decided to take it to a talking level getting to know each other a little more. After a year Pierre decides to move to A.C. so things pretty much didn't work out for them two but they remained friends. Brianna year was almost up, to return back home to her mother, but things change a lot while her mother was in North Carolina dealing with her siblings and the neighborhood. Back in North Carolina my Aunt Ros lived along the roads in Bethel. Aunt Ros is the oldest sister of Felicia and Dee and a child of Clara. January 2006 Baby Najee was born who was the son of Gary. A new little one into the family. Summer 2006 Aunt Dee and the kids took a trip down in North Carolina to visit Aunt Ros in the hospital who was sick very bad. All this family could do was try and stick together. Pulling up in Moyewood neighborhood where Felicia lived, it was around 7pm at the latest. A young girl name Latrice ran up on Brianna crying because of some little boy putting his hands on her. My family remembered her from vacations in the summer time but they didn't know the situation. As kids all Brianna, her cousins and siblings could do was retaliate back. What did it all come out to was someone getting hurt. That next day was a visit to the hospital. There she was lying in her bed as her nieces and nephews, her sister and mother surrounded her with happiness and the now 6 month old Najee into her world. Things weren't getting better and the family was able to see it all. Back in Moyewood the fight gotten worser. The Moyewood neighborhood running back and fourth throwing bottles, cans bats on to our windows as Brinna Grandmother Clara and Aunt Dee sits on the porch with a family member who was living in North Carolina at the time. The family couldn't do nothing but run in the house. Kids yelling Babies crying. Brianna spotted a metal bat all she could do was pick it up and run towards the back door, grandmom clara grab her.

"Wait until your mother gets here"

Brianna was so upset that she was getting annoyed. her mother was at the grocery store food shopping. everything that was brought was left at the store. food getting rung up. In no time There was Gary, Malik, momma Felicia, and Amina who was the mother of Najee. Round two there was another fight but things just didn't end. Three day fight was the worst for this family. Uncle Horace couldn't keep his Felicia and her family down here any longer. By the next morning uncle Horace and Cousin J'L was down to pack and go. The only thing that was an option was to go room in a motel for the night. One day everything had to be out the house, Felicia was so upset Brianna seen the tears in her eyes. She didn't want to leave. Until this day It was our fault because of the way we rushed into trying to hurt someone who disrespect someone who meant the world to them. Back on the road on their way to Jersey. Laughs were shared, evil eyes were twitching, and sadness just showed. Driving with a car full plus a uhal wasn't the best idea but getting away from the pain was the best idea. Lets pray was all the family could do while swerving into a bad car accident that end up coming out into god hands who saved them for another try of happiness. Back in Jersey thing got worse but better. It was July 10th Brianna's birthday, a phone called came in from the New jersey hospital from Aunt dee:

"Aunt Ros might not make it"
"She not leaving on my birthday" Brianna cried out.
Days gotten worse. July 14th 2006 Roslind Knight was pronounced gone.
Where do this family go from here, hatetrate towards each other was what they experience.

At age seventeen Brianna moved in with her dad Shyleer whom she had just meet, was moving in with him meant to be? was all she asked herself. After living with her dad for three months. Brianna realized that at one point she wasted her time even taking that chance but then she thought to herself and said it was the best experience that she had to ever go through. Moving back in with my mother was great. Living in Willingboro Country Club was a little not cool for her, because catching the bus was not in her mind. Back to the pain and haterate and dislikes between the family. When will it all stop was all the family could ask themselves and each other but in meanful ways. Brianna and her mother continued the pain and stressing towards each other. At age 18 year 2007, Brianna thought life would be a little better less rules and maybe a little later curfew, but all of that didn't happen.

One night Brianna decided to walk off her porch to walk around the corner for a few seconds.

The next day her mother and her had gotten into a little conflict about it. That night things gotten worse so Brianna decides to leave and not come back. That night Brianna had no where to go, so the only choice she made was to sleep outside. She found away to get in the house well when it was the next morning. She had to go, her mother wasn't dealing with no disrespectful kids, so that was that. From summer 2007 to December Brianna moved in with a few family until a few days before Christmas. Brianna hated spending Christmas with other families. After moving in with Nick, Brianna felt that she was more home even though her mother and Nick was no longer together. Living there for almost two years wasn't so bad for her. She felt as though she was home. Summer 08 was here it was the best summer but the worst summer. Julian Corry was One of the most popular kid in school and everyone he hung out with. Brianna and many of her friends lost a good Friend Julian who They called Poowie or either King Julian. Julian passed July 18 2008, eight days after Brianna birthday so it was another summer where she just didn't want to have a month of July, but she knew that was out of the question. Brianna and Pierre finally made it together. Loving each other non stop but the pan was kicking into their relationship. Brianna and Pierre Relationship only lasted Four months but it was the best four months she had ever had. Love was no more in Brianna category. Brianna moved on and kept love away from her or as tough she tried. Around December Brianna and Ravon kind of click back with each other but just as friends. After getting to know each other it was like the love thing came back to her. She couldn't help it, but with Ravon it was like he was all she needed well wanted to be with. June 19th 2009 Was the best day for Brianna it was graduation day. Turning 20 July 10th Brianna had a big birthday party plus a graduation party. The house was packed wit so many people. It's 2010 a new year a better Brianna and hopefully a better life.

Was i wrong ?

Momma always told me to be careful who i love
be careful who i choose in and out my life
was i wrong for loving you
Are you the one who deserve to be in my life
was i wrong, was i wrong
i ask myself,
i see something in you
but was i wrong for loving you
if loving you was wrong i know i don't wanna be right
you put me through pain
you put strength in my soul
but was i wrong for loving you
was i wrong
i'm hurt from the pain
but pain is pleasure,
Right?
Tears from stress but it only made me stronger
so was i, was i wrong for
loving you?

dedicated to Ra'von

Times

Times is ruff, times is hard, times been lonely and times been sad
How do i concentrate when your gone, can't focus the right way
Months been dark and bright at times
people getting weak but at times you making them stronger
friends separating, wishing they can come closer
when will i see you again
only god knows
why did you leave this earth so soon
only god knows why
sometimes it feels pointless to sit here in this cold world without you
your advice, your kisses, and your giggles made a lot of us stronger
your jokes and all kept a lot of us going instead of giving up
we miss our king so dearly
family and friends live day by day wishing you were back in our site
watch over us baby boy
we love you.

"R.I.P PoOwie"

I Left

I left the only man who i know would
take the last breath for me
the only man who dreamed of me being the
only women next to him
I left the only man who i know would
get on one knees to make a permit commitment
the only man who really wondered if i'll love him back
i left the only man who i know,
rather if i'm with him or not he'll love every moment we had
than and now
the only man who would take me
far away in his arms and not let go
i left the only man, the only man who
would not give up on me being a friend, a best friend,
his girl or wife
i left, i left, yes i left the only man
of a womens dream.

Love

Love is such a strong word
love is such a deep deep word
love is a word that i once told him
a word that i express
to him with no hesitation
no hesitation at all
The love got deeper, the feelings got stronger
but the pain, the pain turned into tears
he tears turned into happiness
as the happiness got longer
the stronger i got
this pain turned into me still standing and
looking forward into success
but i realize
what make pain make you stronger
Love is such a disease so use it in a healthy way

The Abuse

She came along way
from the abuse
who held her back from success but not love
love is what she needed from the one who's
going to lead her into success not pain
but the love she got was the love of pain
she came so far from the abuse
who seem to not want her mind looking at greatness but hate
hate was what she accomplished
she got it all and he got it all
so why can't she have it all
but greatness
was what she deserve
so she stand tall and look back once and said to herself
"i will not turn back around i will keep walking
till i can't no more"
she walks ahead and never looked back
Greatness accomplished
so now she got it all

dedicated to my aunt dee who never gave up on me

Confidence

I ran from something i thought
was holding me back
from something i believe that was
going to stop me from looking forward
I ran from this person
who i thought wasn't
going to let me live to see another day
who had me crying for years
I ran from this person who had me bleeding
on the inside
but smiling on the outside
why?
I ask,why run from the pain
that'll make you stronger
not only did i ran from you
but from life and the people in it
that made me a better person
No more will i run
i'll face you and life with confidence
because
still i believe i can stand strong
and not fall
No more will i run

Grandmother Clara who kept me going by her stories & love

She's My Everything

When i was Crawling she was there to help me walk
When i was crying she was there to hold me and shed tears
When i was falling she was there to catch me
When i ran from the pain
she was there to tell me to face it and keep my head up
When i'm struggling
she told me success was on it's way
This is why she's my everything
But if i die
i know she'll
keep me and her memories alive

dedicated to my mother Felicia who i love so dearly

Study

It takes time to learn that word
but it takes more time to learn the world
still i don't understand how everything happens
still i wonder and i wonder
but never will i wonder for the future
only time will tell, only time will tell
so i live for today and hope for tomorrow
but still i wonder
how will i ever
understand this world
i write deep thoughts
and i write what i see
i understand
my work but i can't
understand this cold world i live in
scared from time to time
but still i wonder
will i understand
this world
No
so i wonder
will you understand
me?

dedicaated to my two brothers Leek && Strick who seems
to b the ones who understands me more

to my cousin Danicqua K who stayed by myside when things
got ruff i love u neek

• • • •

She only relax herself once in the blue
but when that time comes she think about a lot
how she struggle as a teen
living house to house
shelter homes
friends and family homes
Grew up around the streets
where she knew she would hurt
dangerous men
sick women
she was young on the streets
she was very afraid
around there things got worse
being sexually assaulted
no one to look up to
she hide her tears from all
who surrounded her with joy and happiness
she shared her tears with the pillow and herself
the more she cried
the more she stood
so no more rain drops falling from them stars
unless its happiness and success she accomplish
so she stand till she can't stand no more
She look at herself in the mirror
and the one thing she said
"it's easy to make mistakes but it's hard to learn from them,
but once you learn it'll make you stronger"
still she stand

This Book is dedicated to my:
My mother Felicia
Aunt Dee
Aunt Ros
Grandmom Clara
Gary
Malik
Tawanna
Marniqua
Tylicia
Mikea
Niesha
Nicholas
Najee
Naseem
NakiyahGrandmom MInnie (R.I.P)
NaKiyah
Grandpa William (R.I.P)

Yamir
Chanel
Jaquiera
Jaishon
Tylique
Aunt Dora (R.I.P)
Julian AkA Poowie (R.I.P)
RiQ (R.I.P)
Gilbert (R.I.P)
Fat Man (R.I.P)
Aunt Dianna & family
Shaquan
Uncle Al
Uncle James
danicqua/ nee nee/ ma ryda
muff

ta'shaun
chareese
zahir
Kristen
Sdot
steve
tony
Damian

Kateena D
Smuve
Geeze
frenchie
loose
Ashley/ dimples
aunt marqaret
shanika
marc
jasmine
sylvia
Kelz
Ky
Telaiya
Danny
Dalyn
E-Nitty
Dez
Chareese M & Zay
Kiara .P
Dane
Court
Mesha
Aunt Carol
Uncle Danny

Pete & Shy
Danicqua A
Rachelle
Kellee
Kyleesa
shannon
ky
aniah
serenity
damir
kylah
kysir
kylee
lisa
Juan
Rob N
ZaQuanna
Malik
Quil
Kay
Jelani
Shabash
Streetz

Teeyana
Tim
Kamiyla
Aunt Fannie
danielle
valerie
Evan
Keith
Joshua
Mariah

Courtney
Uncle Leon
Uncle Horace
Aunt Darlene
LiL Horace
Phillip
Jarvis
Nick
Latrice
Mrs Shebbie
Tory
E-Nitty
Dez
ashaunte aka shaun shaun
toya
jessie
malachi aka bronx
martha aka bootsie
ricky aka slick rick
Russel
Peanut
Pop Off

danielle, twins' & sionney mone`t . . . bless yu
NaQuanna
milyra & prince kai
Mel
Aunt Tank
Aunt Lorinda
Gmom. Mary
Shyleer
Ranada
Trashan
Brandon

Blair
Beverly
Kylah
Amare'
Quasim
pareese
mama
marcus jr
Tynisha N.
Shank Daddy
Tra
Jas B.
Alleah Carter & Kimberly
Fly Bul Gene
Kwaseem
Day'Day
Kinesha; Nesh
Brandi
Darnelle
Charmaine (R.I.P)
Mica
~MZ.PRETTY~
Shakila aka Killa
C.J.
Danielle aka D.Lee
hector aka Hec boog
Marcelus aka Fel aka Celus
Janelle Jenkins
Cassandra Little (R.I.P)
breezy burner
Drae/Zues
Jordan, Jada, & Don Juan
ashli renee'
Kendal nadine

Teflon Don
shaquana miriam
Jose aka "jos" aka KillaJos aka ya bro
Tempeste
chavana, (bessie)
deborah
alana
dequan
jaelyn
davion
Chareese aka mamaz
Preston

Jasmine Danielle
Bryanna Freeming

KJ Baggett
chris juan barnes
will franklin
Bilal
Ameir
Azeir
Duce
Shamar
B
ho ho
twork
fresh
speedy
don breez
ern mac
trae poundz
Umpa
Tajanete

Ayana
Dom Gotti
Raquell
Chance
Asane
ashli renee'
Quameya Nashe
Davonte Jones
Davon jones
Tara JONES
Mushy

Charles
berry
andrew

leafy
Dom Pom.!!
Nyla london*
bstrick
LaLa
Court bundlezzzzz
Dom.H
Keisha H
Jaz
Star
Shaky
cony's
Rob
S.Little
Tiff

JDOGG
ManMan

Bay
Duke
Keedy
Chug
Naeem
Boobie
Rendal
RAY RAY
Andre

Mally G
Aknellz!!!!!
RuGa Rellz
Kris C & JuJu
Tiana
Poowie aka King Julian
J.R.
Kirb
Jeremy
Denis
indigo
Ci. Nicole

Nakeisha Lashae.
trell aka trizzy
Brianca
Nicole
Tony
Robyn
Jazz
Tia
Kiana
Mike-Mike
MarQuise

sheree
andre
anthony
chico
deshaun
kalil
mikah
Andrew

David
Robert
Mae
Audrey
Angela
Rj
Raffi &
Beatrice
Milton
ATL shawty
Bk.
ur boy irv ~yung fre$h~

QUANA * MS. SWEET N LOVELY*
ray ru bka ray mickens
Najee
suzie f. babyy. ▪
danielle
mandy
dj
dezmone bka dez &&& aaliyah the princess"

angela && baby ka'shuan && Carlton Whte
Keyona, Anthony, && Romaine
Tim :)

AignYeezy! (Yeh)
Jarmay, Jarmaz, n phil
Deylan Jenkins aka Dey Dey
Ki MaCk
Brian Xavier Richardson

elijah "ya ya" barnes
Ta'Jah aka Tayj,
Ajanae' aka Aj,
Amoni aka Moni
Tashianna
Tanisha
Glen
Doris
Renisha
Tasheeda
Kiara k
Trese
Popii
sheema
ashly
mummers
Rell k
Tylique (Twins)
Jaqueria
Jaishon
Chanel
T-pain
Brianna k
shaun & wayne
Beamer
Rell k
Dacelle
Kishara aka Choc ▪

Chris aka Mr.Swaggd Up
Daniel lamaar jeremyah jefferies . . . .
alrick aka Slick~rick
Chanaye, Milan.
Pierre
Renisha
Kathy
Smack
Snodgrass

Kinjite bka taye baby jada
kesh alexandre., congrats!
myasia (mymy)
Ron Coney
Kim. C (weiirdo)
taylour; tay • yu.
ebecca; or becca or bec . . . congratss bri!!! =]
angelo aka babes
tom aka fav white boy
Cierre Symone
Tiara W
C.Pierce
Traffic
heem aka trillz aka trillavel
Cindy
Chantel
De'Asia
Arius
John S
Arlethia & NAdir
Shelly
Victoria
tiara
Static

Daemen
Jnean
Jaz
Jabri
Terrance
Frankie
brenda
munchy
Kirk
Marcus M
Brianna
Ayo
Ashley Cierra
Tee-Kay
angel
Anissa
Brandon. H
Antoine .C
Gerald d
Lamar M
Demetrius
Romeka
Bria .Y Brittany
Avery
Carwell
Deeze
Tahira
Justin
Dashayn
Danyra
dana
TAmmy
Akeya
Lexis

Barry
Chelsea
chris m.
cerise
gary
Antwine
Smuve
Mook
Cornell
keyshita
Brandon
Scrap
wolf
d.lum
Ghost
Lenard
E.Pistol
Mook
Sabrina
Tetta
Tiff
Pip
Worm (RIP)
Quise
Sam
Catlyn
Cassandra

Starlicious
Dave AKA Noodles
Ofiicer: Robert Boyd
Chanel Znane'
Shaquielle Butler
Jarquan McCurry

Jakeera McCurry
Adam Sign
Lashay Page (Mrz Star)
Shanikwa K Brinson
Aniya M
Mia Fussel
Catera
Lance
Tyrell H
Zadaya Nieves
~L.I.E~
~F.O.E~

Made in the USA
Middletown, DE
02 April 2022

63527179R00056